MY JOURNEY:

The Loss of a Loved One

by

Helen Napoli Cabrera

MY JOURNEY:
The Loss of a Loved One

by

Helen Napoli Cabrera

April, 2003

Raven Press

10.11.05
Dear Liz,
It is great
to feel that
I have touched
another with
my writing
Love,
Helen
(Marie)

My inspiration for this piece of my life came as a need to tell of my loneliness and loss of my loved one. A need so great that this work is full of truth and a reaching out to those who are experiencing the same pain.

I am the mother of two sons, blessed with six grand-children and have lived in Old Greenwich, Connecticut, for thirty-two years. This is a very important part of my life.

Believing in myself as a poet, understanding my need to reach out and enjoying the love that surrounds me are the reasons for smiling!

hnc

Contents

Preface

Here, take my hand. Go with me, share my pain. Grief has stolen many precious hours, but feel my awakening. Traveling with me you will get to know me. I will share my every emotion so that you can relate and within yourself find hope to accompany you on your journey. I will introduce you to the life I shared with Jim. It will enable you to know me as a real person, someone who has felt what you are feeling.

This book has been written over a three-year period, the time needed for this journey to begin, to reach the end of this particular journey, and then for the opening of another horizon, the rest of my life. I have the need to tell you that we are not alone, to reach out and share, to make you understand that what you are feeling and the tears you are crying are my emotions also. I know. I have walked in your shoes.

*The loss of my husband could not be measured on a scale of one to ten. If you have lost that person so dear, then you are experiencing the agony I wish to address. It was so heartbreaking that I felt I would never mend. In my piece, **I Arrived On Wounded Wing** I wrote, "that what was, still is." When I wrote that line, I knew that Jim was dead, will never again be beside me, but that I had to continue.*

*As you read what I have written, know that I am sharing where I have been with you. May this enable you to cry harder, dry your tears and take heart in the value of all the tomorrows to come. You will again find a time and place of inner peace. Hold on, dear reader. Take my hand. Please walk with me as I tell you of **My Journey.***

4.14.00

Chapter I   September 30, 1997
The Beginning of My Journey

My life seemed to end. My husband, my love and best friend, was gone. Out of my grief I was able to compose **That Summer of '97**. It came to me during one of the many sleepless nights that followed his death. It was a song that I sang into the night. It was a lament. It was a reaching out to all who loved Jim. It was my tribute to the man I loved, the man who shared forty-three years of my life, forty-one years in marriage.

The writing was sent to our dear friend and artist, David Armstrong. He painted the eagle even though he was very ill. My gratitude for his friendship, so often extended, has now fully blossomed as his extraordinary talent helped produce a unique and loving memorial card. Seven hundred cards were mailed throughout the world. Jim Cabrera was loved and respected by so many. He will be missed forever.

He Left On Eagle's Wings

The summer of '97

*My true love soared to unbelievable heights using
Bravery and courage to guide him*

The summer of '97

Their father viewed mountains we have yet to climb

The summer of '97

Our friends majestically touched our hearts

The summer of '97

His love and devotion feathered our nest

The summer of '97

At breath of dawn he saw his children's children play

The summer of '97

His spirit gracefully landed atop the highest peak

The summer of '97

Then a blazing September sunset marked his farewell to:

That summer of '97

hnc

I found some solace by putting my feelings on paper. Full heart-rending thoughts, thoughts that were shared with my two sons and their families. I told them how much I loved Jim and what I was planning, planning to go on. I did not know what path to take. Not aware of the hazards of being alone and deep in grief, I still wanted to strike out and find some type of happiness. Not wanting to burden my family with hours of dialogue, I penned a piece, **And, Then He Was Gone**, to be read on my birthday in March, almost six months after Jim's death. It brought tears as I read the words, but I hoped that they would understand that I was going to go on. It was a tribute to our marriage when their response was, "We understand. Try to find happiness. But, please be careful." I think they realized how vulnerable I was, and I realized that they were still experiencing deep grief. As always, our love and our lifelines were open and caring. This was like gathering all my ducks, putting them in line, and then stepping back and reflecting. Another step to wellness. Read and see if you can identify.

And, Then He Was Gone

It is a hard task to "be well"...as all my family and friends lovingly advise me to "take care" as they leave me to continue their day's work, their lives, lives that now no longer include my husband and myself, because my husband is no longer with me, he has gone.

I am left, loneliness is a difficult companion. Loneliness fills every corner of every dark room, even though I have turned on every light in the room...the room remains dark. Difficult, also when you have to find this room bright when people who love you and have loved your husband occupy your space, your room. So you turn on your brightest lights to help them not see the darkness that has become your life, and for them not to worry, lights are lit, smiles forced and you reach down for the strength to put up a "good front." The glow of their love helps for a while after they leave, but before you know it...the room is dark again.

How can I find myself again, that self that was always a half of a whole, now only a half...but the need to be whole again? Give thanks...I ask for what?...and then one day, in the glare of today, a candle is lit and the wonder of the light from one candle illuminates the memories that are tucked in corners and I start to say "thank you"...thank you for the years, the memories, the children, the love I felt...for being you...and tomorrow is upon me.

Remember..."Helen, it's been a good ride!" I feel that way too. It was a wonderful ride, full of highs and lows, full of smiles and tears, full of sharing and selfishness, full of triumphs and defeats...but always full of us. And now I face tomorrow by myself, or so I thought, as I venture out of my dark room accompanied by a lone lit candle. You will always be with me, at my side. You have taught by example as you tasted with aplomb the joys of the world around you.

Your friends...you showed me how to be a good friend, how to care when it was easier for me to retreat into myself and not share. You never were gentle with your teachings, for you never taught, you just gave me a push and said, "You can do it"...and then went on to explain how easy it would be to be a friend. All your friends have become my world and because of you and what you were, they are giving me the comfort I need, thank you.

Your class...it was as much a part of you, so naturally so, as your not wearing socks, getting lunch on your ties and being proud of it, your red hankie, a tear in your pants (so what) and to carry it off with such panache that success found you...and you shared it with me, always giving me credit for being there for you. I remember it was never a direct compliment, rather an off-centered comment that made me feel good all over...the same feeling of pride and passion as I viewed your walk (could recognize it a mile away) everyday during those forty-three years.

Your love...how was I to know what that love would encompass? How could I tell about the future we were to share when all I wanted was you---your attention, your opinions and, of course, your body! We were the talk of the campus because I could not keep my hands to myself when I was near you. How was I to know that you would be the best Father that our two boys could have... how was I to know the joy I felt when you interacted with your grandchildren...how was I to know you would respect and accept my family...how was I to know that we would ever have more than the $50 we started with...how was I to know that the next 43 years would take us to all parts of the world...how was I to know how lucky I was to find you? I know now, and bless every minute that I shared how fortunate we were every time I could get you to really listen to my thoughts..."times up" can still be heard!!

Your face...I will never forget your face nor your sense of humor. You will never grow old for me, nor will you ever lose your laugh... It will remain in my heart forever.

Your dreams...have been realized. I remember you telling me that when you die no one will have any regrets because you lived everyday the way you chose to...your way! I was so happy to see you a success as a businessman...I saw your dreams realized...and they still live in the hearts of all your friends and family.

Your courage...your illness took my breath away. I look back now and I cannot remember breathing for days. I prayed for God's help so that you could become my Jim again. He didn't answer. As I relive those months I realize He heard me... He gave you the courage to fight with the bravery that I shall never see again...nor will most people ever be able to repeat your finest hour. I say your finest hour, because if you had not been so brave I could not have held your hand and believed in our love and not questioned this terrible illness that stole you away from me. Your unquestioning strength will carry me along this road until I am with you again.

As I take my memories and tie them with a lavender silk ribbon and hug them to my breast, I will smile through my tears as I say, "walk with me"...I want to leave the darkness and walk toward the rainbow that represents the rest of my life. Only when someone has been given so much, can they take the journey of the next years with confidence and assurance...the joy of our life together will make the years to come possible, thank you...

Until tomorrow, my love.

March 10th, 1998

Our professional life was so full. I was a wife who shared every phase of Jim's corporate life. His love for life spilled over to his job. There was a personal relationship with his clients and a total familiarity with staff, my life became filled with these people. Letters received daily after Jim's death told me of their loss. So many stories, so many memories. When I was asked to attend a conference dedicated to my husband by his company, I was elated. "Would you like to participate?" "Yes, oh yes", and the piece **Music** was created.

After I had **Music** in its final draft, I read and reread what I had written. Another small forward motion as our life spoke to me from the page. It was a time of full attention to my words, a total reflection. There were six hundred colleagues in the audience, and not a dry eye. A tear fell often and rightly so, for it was still too soon to face my loss.

Even though I had shared my piece, my peace still was not a part of me. I left friends and associates to go home, alone. I prayed for the hurt to subside. That is when I cried out for an avenue of self-help and I found a winding country road: writing poetic prose. The process of finding peace was continuing.

MUSIC......our life together, Jim's and mine, was set to music. All types, from his classical to my pop, but always in sync, well, almost always in sync. It started at Rider College, now Rider University. That was the intro to the symphony of life that now remains unfinished, but a truly wonderful, loving piece of work.

I can remember our first song...I can still hear him singing "Teach me tonight" into my ear...and teach me he did, in so many ways. Together we learned to be husband and wife, father and mother, in-laws, grand-parents, good friends, loyal corporate mates , but mostly we were in tune with each other. We each marched to our own drummer, but when we danced he always did his two step...sometimes fast, sometimes slow...and I was able to follow his lead.

The King and I and The Sound of Music could be heard on our 45 as we were producing our own musical...known for years as the Cabrera Clan or the Flying Cabreras (when Joe and Jimmy took their great athletic prowess to the golf course, how the men in my life loved to play golf together...even though they refused to give me a stroke a side!)...some-times it was musical comedy but mostly the stage of our home was filled with love and friendship.

Then came the production company...Drake Beam...the financial back-ers that enabled our musical to go on the road. Our home in Old Greenwich, Columbia and Duke educations, travel and memberships to golf clubs...this all made the beat of the music faster...the vibrato rich-er...a fuller interruption...and played as loudly as the speakers would allow. It was the time of Man of LaMancha with Richard Killey at the Vivian Beaumont Theater......a time when we would start to gather the strength to fight the windmills of the future.

It was at 277 Park on the 7th floor that John Drake and Jerry Beam, along with Gladys and Gertrude welcomed Jim and myself into the recording studio. A small studio, but the sounds were music to Jim's ears. President of Drake Beam, Executive Search...no less than a tango beat. From there to right here...and the beat goes on.

The Cabrera musical would add skirts (as my son, Jim, so sweetly named the two new women members of our band) and 1/2 notes to our sheet music (in the measure of six grandchildren) our score became more intrinsic and diversified. Three families all dancing to different drummers, but all to the beat of Jim's two step......at times fast, at times slow......but always together. Our first grandson, Jimmy, at age three, shouted on a New York bound train...."Look a picture of Poppy's friend, Pavarotti," much to the amusement of the commuters.....or Tyler, our second grandson, announcing as he entered our car..."What will it be, Poppy's LaBoheme, or Nanny's Dirty Dancing?"

The marketing of our music came in the guise of business. Jim's upbeat personality, his love of his fellow man, his loyalty to Drake, Beam, Morin, his true caring for the staff, but always his own inside music...the song that he played everyday of his life...the song of joy of being JCC...that music marketed the idea of outplacement...an idea that was to change the lyrics of a torch song to a pop hit...the tune all of you hear when the phone rings and a voice says...Good Morning, DBM."

The many conferences...slash...dance music. Here I learned the electric slide, donned a Texas hat for line dancing and danced with everyone...but, when Sinatra's "New York, New York" was played, he knew where to find me...it was our dance, Jim's and mine...just as New York was his city.

Jim two-stepped to the podium, what a great MC. He loved giving out the awards, telling his jokes, and remembering everyone's name and a little jazz about the recipient. His repertoire of "remember whens" could fill this room just as strains of Phantom of the Opera seem to as I look out upon the faces of the DBMers here tonight and remember all the DBMers who sat here before you. I hear refrains from the piano bar...happy songs sung to you by a happy man.

Our song "Moonglow" brings a tear to my eye every time it is played, the piano's refrains of "Ice Castles" make me remember...but I must now share one secret with you...I cannot carry a tune, Jim would say, "Helen, can you just hum."... would poke him, smile and know he was so right. But I will share this with you...He taught me to sing, on key, from my heart.

I know Jim is here with us tonight, I know he would give you all a thumbs up on today and the future of DBM......and I know he would love you to see a thumbs up......here it is.........Thank You.

At the grave...............1999

To Touch was just a small, almost silent prayer. It was at my fingertips often during the next few months. Having memorized the piece, its recitation made my reaching for the light at the end of the tunnel seem a reality. You can almost feel the dread at going on. Why could I not find contentment in my children and grandchildren? The guilt that I could not be helpful to others, the realization that for the first time in my life I was not able to accomplish my wish, to be of value; I started to search. You may understand the restlessness, understand the sadness in believing that you may never be touched again.

To Touch......

It is the feeling of joy
To be touched by your grandchildren.

It is the feeling of remembering
To be touched by your aging parents.

It is the feeling of redemption
To be touched by your God.

It is the feeling unforgettable
To be touched by your lover.

It is the sharing of feelings
To be touched by your friends.

It is that loss of feeling
Never to be touched again.

The feeling of death.

hnc
11.98

Chapter II   Climbing the Mountain

My instincts told me that I must get on with my life. It had been a tough battle with Jim's cancer. My strength had been sapped. I can remember the doctors telling me to care for myself. I now decided that I would get on...and get on I did. After dating again, I wrote **Somewhere in Georgia**. I felt a connection to healing, someone cared. That feeling made me alive again. The most unbelievable things began to happen. I saw and felt a connection to my life with Jim at every turn, in a phrase or a view or even in my stories: i.e. we were in Ireland and...It brought sadness to my conversation, but being able to speak about my life with Jim was healing to me. Friends started to remember incidents, and so life continued.

Then that someone in Georgia ended our relationship. I had never been rejected before. I wonder if I had been sixteen if it would have hurt so badly, but wounded and not sure, I pulled myself up. It was not an easy task. The questions I asked myself were many. I thought I had found a companion, I was wrong. Being wrong does not help heal the soul, it just brings tears and frustration. Combine that with grief, and things were grim.

I stopped writing poetry and put pen to paper telling the world how much I missed that special person, my husband, someone who would never have hurt me. The paragraphs told of pain, how he never said "good bye", my fears of being alone, even words of dying. My sleep was interrupted with "what ifs" and I did not know if I could climb above this latest event. I had reached an impasse. I questioned my ability to go on!

Somewhere In Georgia

What of today, tomorrow and yesterday?
Can they only be shadows of themselves...
When you are grieving?
Are they unreachable, this reality of time...
When you are grieving?
Are they actually happening, are the calendar days really here....
Or are they just struck from the page, not really here
And is here too unbearable!

Then someone again shares today!
What yesterday wrought is a memory,
What tomorrow will bring is a mystery
The sharing has lessened the pain
The shadows drift away and
A tender touch helps to heal.

hnc
3.98

Still very vulnerable, but beginning to see the beauty around me I wrote **The Grey Lady** on a scrap of paper. I was vacationing in Nantucket with someone I was dating. It was a time of involvement and repose from the grief that seemed to be with me twenty-four hours a day. The island of Nantucket is off the coast of Massachusetts, its nickname is the Gray Lady and the zip code is 02554. It is an island that speaks to you. I was ready to listen.

Away from my everyday surroundings, I found I was in a place where I could shed my mantel of grief. I could hear and smell and see and feel again. It was a time of relaxation. A time to heal a little, and then...that relationship also ended. As in every event in your life, some good must come of it. It was on this beautiful island that I was given some encouragement about my writing. How it touched and how I could bring a smile and maybe I had some talent. I wanted to share my songs. Time was helping me over this hurdle, my ability to pour out my heart enabled me to compete in the race, the race of everyday living.

Even though I did not want to race, did not want to compete, did not want to share, my personality gave me the ability to write and ask others to read. I even would read you my "stuff" if you would sit still for only a moment. I needed to reach out. Try reaching, it is healing.

The Gray Lady

The lady in gray stands alone.
Her particled shroud of cooling mist
Protecting her natural beauty.

She stands alone
In a sea of turbulent storms,
Lazy summer days,
Sunsets and sunrises of awesome quality,
Mystical cloud formations and
Prolific flora.

The murmur of her soul can be heard.
In the acclamations of her visitors,
The bellowing of the ferry whistle as it arrives and departs,
In the whining winds of the beaches and bogs,
By the watering of gardens so beautiful
The chiming as metal meets mast at rest in her harbor.

Her sights and sounds are a symphony
Played to the beat of wonderful memories held so dear,
As the gray lady hugs our precious,

Nantucket,

To her breast.

hnc
7.4.98
Place: 02554

Photo taken by Joan Kadlec   2001

Chapter III Verifying the Route

When I first wrote **And, Then He Was Gone**, God was not mentioned. I wanted to explain to my sons the faith I knew was within, but how? It was obvious to me (for had I not tended the rosary during hard times) that I did believe in God, but I needed some guidance. A dear friend insisted I try talking to a minister she knew. (Friends reaching out) Being Catholic I questioned, but I will forever be grateful that I made an effort.

This man of the cloth enabled me to tell of my faith to my family, and he held out a hand and listened. His advice and personal beliefs were the stabilizing influence in my life. I had read many books about the loss of one's spouse, the focal point was faith and its ability to heal. I had to find mine again. Bob opened the door.

When I first met Bob I wrote **A Calling**. I know it was my way of saying thank you in a very personal way. I was beginning to share my need. I attended bible study classes and had counseling sessions which prompted **To: Whom It May Concern**. I was doing it my way. When my English friends (both of whom had lost spouses and were concerned about me) responded to a particularly grim day with "Have you seen your vic'r lately?", I immediately found focus and wrote "The Vic'r". The piece enabled me to state that I was beginning to feel at home in a church setting. I even began to wear my hats again. A small personal identity, feeling a part but yet still me. Putting myself together again. It seemed as though it was one step forward and although I might encounter a half step back, I was still plowing ahead, slowly. (Can you feel my need to be well again?)

I began to realize the joy in observing others. **A Woman's Way** fed my creative being on this special Sunday. A smile could not be suppressed as my mind flew to how I would put this to music. So much for the sermon. My concentration has never been wonderful, but when beautiful messages formed in my mind, I decided to listen. Another small step.

A Calling...

He extended his hand in a greeting...

His eyes reflected the warmth of his interest...

A smile conveyed his sincerity...

His voice, filled with compassion, spoke his name...

We shared a handshake...

I dropped a tear in welcome...

Then, a caring embrace to quiet my fears...

And as arms held life so fragile...

A friendship was born.

Thank you.

Thank you.

hnc
3.14.98

To: Whomever it may concern
Re: Character Evaluation
Objective: Promotion to Senior Spokesman

Do I see Him in Gucci loafers?
Does He wear Ferragamo ties?
Does He dine at 21?
Does He drive a Jaguar?
What is His address?
Have I asked about his education?
Or
Have I just felt His presence recently?
Have I not cared about his appearance?
Have I not cared about the trappings of success?
Have I wanted to embrace just the sandaled feet,
The quiet manner,
The coarse robe,
The crude table set with just bread and wine,
The promise of contentment,
The special feeling of being loved without reservation,
The absence of prejudice,
The love of son for mother,
The giving of mutual respect without full understanding,
The knowing He is listening?
So
I have been introduced to an old friend,
I knew His Mother, Mary, far better,
She helped me to know His work,
Understand His word
Love Him through her eyes
Now
I feel His work and word
I want to learn more about Him
And
I see Him as He sees me
Without any trappings,
Just me, just Him.

Recommendation: Go with it, offer Him the job. He has great potential.

hnc 3.23.98

VIC'R

My English friends refer to him as the Vic'r.
Some church members call him their minister.
Referred to as a priest, elder or rabbi.
More often than not, a man of the cloth.
All the above spoken with reverence
For men who represent their God.

He stands before you on the Sabbath.
A moral pillar whose values are unquestionable.
A role model, one who sees his faults,
So very special in communicating his sameness.
Offering an answer with a question.
Being there within the vestments of the order.

But the pulpit stands apart.
The bible feels heavy in your hands
As the words are read with reverence.
Your understanding is paramount, for
A mind is the tablet whereupon the stylus marks
The words of yesterday, spoken today.

The bridge over the waters of time.
Vic'r, minister, priest, rabbi, elder, man of the cloth,
He or she architecturally designs the span.
The knowledge of text, logic abounds
And, you travel not only to enlightenment
But, to a place of contentment.

Is it the clear eyes that bind?
The vision they see?
Could it be the resonance of the voice?
Heard in the singing of Him
Yes, but it is the gesture that awakens,
Calling an awareness of voice and eyes.

The hands extend in greeting.
They embrace the book they carry.
They warm the shoulders of the weary.
They clasp the face of the forlorn.
They welcome the faithful and those of little faith.
They become the beacon in the dark.

Caring and loving are these hands.
Healing of spirit is accomplished by an embrace,
Two hands steady a falling soul.
Stilled in pockets ready to express concern or
Gently touching the cross on the bosom
While listening with full attention.

Be called to serve, those hands, that heart,
By whatever name.
You hear the wails of those assembled.
You measure the importance of one sheep.
You share His word and His love.
You administer kindness and understanding.

Know I am listening to your words of wisdom,
Making my grief tolerable.
Know I hear the choir's message,
Enabling my voice to sing.
Know I feel at home in His house,
Renewing the belief that I am a beloved guest.

Thank you, dear Vic'r.

hnc
3.6.00

A Woman's Way

Ministry on a beach in September
Cloudless sky colored blue by design
Needy and giving congregation with bowed heads

Then...

A child with gifts to bear
Scattered sand from busy feet
Dirty hands cradling three cherished stones

Shhhh from Father...smile from Mother

Windblown hair shading sparkling eyes gifting
One stone for Father, two stones for Mother
Retreating brown arms and legs flying

Then...

Silently Father places stone on sand
Mother views the special find and
Lovingly stows them in her bag

For...

Precious is this gift...this child.

hnc
9.98

Chapter *IV* *Arriving at the Peak*

I could not believe that one year had passed since Jim's death. Marking an anniversary such as this was very awakening. I would rather be marking our 43rd wedding anniversary, disbelief whispered in my ear. I did not want to mark this day, it made me see reality. One year, oh my God!

As I stood at the gravesite with my children and grandchildren, listening to the words read, the pain was almost unbearable. I had written **The Hanging of Hearts** to accompany the actual act of placing sparkling hearts on two small Japanese split-leaf red maple trees that flanked the grave. A blanket of beautiful flowers sat atop the grave. There were lavender and white roses, white lilies, tiny purple orchids, white stock, and two beautiful orchids at the center. His grandchildren took some roses and held them and later placed them on the grave. As my daughter-in-law read the poem, hearts were hung and tears flowed. We were to take pictures so that I could make a scrapbook for us to share later. When they were developed we realized that Tyler, my 10-year old grandson, was not in the pictures. I then wrote from my heart. I would also like to share **Tyler's Tears** with you. The grief process is so unbelievably difficult.

The Hanging of Hearts

To hang your heart on a tree is for one to see
That your love for Poppy will forever be.

They sparkle so true as the sun sends a ray
Only makes us believe in the joy of today.

As the smile we remember lights up your life
His boys, his cookies, his pumpkins, the skirts, his wife.

We will always remember as he held us, so dear
That beat of his heart sending good cheer.

So love with a passion those gathered this day
Love with understanding, his listening way.

Never shall his touch be gone from our face
And the warmth of his arms in his good -bye embrace.

hnc
9.30.98

Tyler's Tears

To mark the first anniversary of Poppy not being
with us, we, his loving family, held a service at
his gravesite. In this album are pictures of this
day. Everyone is pictured except our Tyler...I do
not know why his face is missing, but his heart
swelled to overflowing as Tyler's tears joined with
mine on this anniversary. I held him in my arms
as the other grandchildren felt his pain. Eyes of
blue and brown offered him love. Anguish twist-
ed that beautiful face, so like his Grandfather's, as
the tears trailed through the sprinkling of freck-
les onto my bosom. I wish I could have taken the
hurt away, dried those tears and made a smile
touch his lips...I could not, for Poppy is gone.
Growing up is so hard, but as we all grow and
experience life, his voice will reach out and be
heard telling us that all will be fine...just do your
best.

After a breakfast of pancakes, Poppy's favorite, I
returned to view the flowers and say a special, "I
miss you", when a Monarch butterfly arrived
and landed on the blanket. You will see this won-
der in the picture. My memory will always see
us hanging hearts, leaving personal drawings
and painted rocks at the gravesite.

hnc
9.30.98

Photo taken by Helen Cabrera 9.30.9

This day signaled the end of the chronological journey, the three-year anniversary of Jim's death. I still have the days until my personal life's journey end, but I marked this day with a rose bookmark. We met as a family at the gravesite. White lilies and red roses reflected in the ebony stone bearing our family name and the beautifully etched eagle.

I read Matthew, Chapter 18:10 thru 14. I wanted to tell our sheep that even though we love each and every one of them, that if one is lost I will look until I find them. I also read the bible's definition of a rose. We then each said a prayer and placed a rose on the grave.

It amazes me that I can get through a day like this, filled with so much emotion and love, but as we travel the road our desire to reach our destination gives us strength we never knew we had. The need and the want to travel on were so insistent on that day.

hnc
9.30.00

The Meaning of a Rose

Hold the rose, this red rose
Think of what it represents.
For me the past, pleasant memories.
It begins as the Rose of Delta Sigma Pi
Continues in my wedding bouquet
Accenting with fragrance the years till now.

The hands that today hold roses
Belong to those we love.
Names like Jim, Ty, Brooke,
Peter, Katie and Jake.
All roses in our bouquet of life
The centerpiece for our table.

They will bloom and flourish,
These flowers of our union.
They do bring happiness and pride
Joy, laughter and contentment.
As the years pass and tomorrow comes
I will await their full bloom.

Place, today, here with me
Our promise to look to the future.
To try our best with today and
Know Poppy's love is with us forever.
Appreciate the beauty of the rose
Love each other in God's name,

And,

That if God has taken the time to fashion this beautiful rose
He will find time to listen to your prayers.
As you hold this rose in the palm of your hand
Know that He will always hold you in the palm of His hand.

hnc
9.30.00

Our grandchildren   1

Chapter V   A Sunset, Day's End

Doing my best to care, trying to be a good person, never really thinking in depth of friendship, I moved along with a smile and an occasional frown. Death and what it does to people was not a concern. Up to this point I had never felt the devastation caused by death. Now being there, my compassion reached heights never before fathomed. How could I tell my feelings to those who have loved and lost? I know, by writing. By singing my thoughts, by sharing my love through my writing I could reach out and touch. So began the series of poems meant to hug the families left to cry, I could now hug with understanding. Words alone were not enough. They had to be in the form of a tribute. I would do my best to comfort by letting them know I cared.

David Armstrong was such a talent. Finding joy in his painting and love in his friendship was delightful. It was an evening of learning to be with him. Fortunate enough to be at his dinner table, to be in New York at the Hammer Gallery surrounded by his work, to see him open his new barn gallery on Beaver Creek in Pennsylvania, to view his work in my home, to hear his voice on the phone...all this brought a new dimension to my appreciation of art. David made the world of paint and brush alive for me. His ability to see, feel and share was extraordinary. His illness and subsequent death hit with such impact that it was almost unreal.

Our David was penned as I tried to embrace all that he meant to me...what I saw in his work...reach out to his daughter, son and father. Time to put my grief aside and face the grief of others. It is possible.

Last Run Watercolor by David Armstrong 194

Our David

He was broad of jaw
Sandy hair that fell on forehead
Eyes of the softest color
Voice that spoke with gentleness.

His hands were expressive
They were his instruments
His fingers were finely tuned
As his vision directed the miracle.

His laughter could be heard
Among the treed slopes of Pennsylvania
Midst the flapping of sheets
And the melting of Spring snow.
His friendship can be felt
Through true characterization on canvas
The lined faces of his subjects
Showed thought and understanding.

He gave so much of himself
To his craft
To his family
To his friends
To his college
To his community
To the world.

He placed within those who touched
And those who viewed
That special love
Of the beauty that his eyes were to see.

His breath may never be felt again
As he leaned to whisper a thought
His soft touch a thing of yesterday
As we remember a welcoming hug.

He will always be with us:
In our memories
In our hearts
In his work
In a basket of berries
In the red of a bow
In the babble of a brook
In the strength of a quarter horse
In the laziness of a sleeping dog
In the loneliness of a forgotten sleigh
In the ebbing winter sun
In the austere rocks of a shoreline
In the blue of a sky
In the warmth of a nestled home
In the memories that bring us close to

Our David

hnc
11.29.98

John and Jane were a couple who loved each other. During the time of John's illness, my sense of compassion gave Jane a lifeline. She knew she could call me anytime to cry, to talk, to ask advice. This was my first encounter with helping a friend deal with the arrival of death. I knew that nothing I could say would make it better, just being there to listen was my assignment. At times I cried also, I could relate to the hopelessness. We would meet in the supermarket and hugs and tears were all we could accomplish. That was fine, we both felt that bond. It is a hard time. How can you pray for someone to die?...so you pray that everyday can be tolerated. That the toll being taken is not too damaging. Then death, and a part of you is gone.

I arrived at the memorial service and was in awe of this beautiful, simple church. Above the altar hung a cross that overpowered the altar. It kept my attention, made me focus. Then beneath this cross I watched his sons and friends eulogize John. It was moving, I wanted to reach out and tell Jane I understood her pain. I did, I wrote **Beneath The Cross** for Jane. It was a hand in friendship.

Photo taken by Helen Cabrera 2001

Beneath the Cross

An Autumn morning.
The sun glistened through the clear windows.
It haloed itself on the heads of those present.
It was mourning.

No shadow did the cross cast.
No ornaments adorned its outstretched arms.
No visual bricabrac to hold it aloft
As though Faith alone, held it wondrously high and secure.

A Faith questioned today by grief.
A Faith needed today to heal a broken heart.
A Faith needed as Mother consoles Son.
A Faith apparent as Son adores Father.

Beneath this Cross
Beneath crosses everywhere
Faith comes to minister.
Faith becomes a necessity.

Sometimes it cannot be found.
Sometimes in the hurt and loss, it seems to vanish.
That miracle so needed was not granted,
Why did He not listen, where was He?

We sing His praise.
Music fills our soul.
The beauty of song sent to heal.
But where was He?

Beneath the Cross
At the crossroad of your life
When you so desperately needed Him,
Where was He?

As the sun touches a hand in gesture
And the tears streak our cheeks
Love is remembered, emotionally shared,
Revealing His presence.

Spoken words,
Past moments told,
Loving embraces remembered,
He has been with us.

Beneath this cross
We relive a life now quieted.
Beneath this Cross
We shed our tears.

When the loneliness becomes unbearable
Remember this day, beneath the Cross.
When it is hard to breathe,
Remember the words spoken, beneath this Cross.

And, if running will not let you reach your destination
And words will not comfort you
And those around you do not fill that terrible void,
Reach deep inside for courage.

You are not alone.
You have your health.
You have his life reflected in your sons.
You have memories to lead you into tomorrow.

Go find happiness.
Go make others smile.
Go accomplish what you do best.
Go knowing he is beside you.

Take my hand,
Use my shoulder, dear friend.
Understand His will, when possible.
Rely on your inner strength.

For beneath this Cross,
On this day of representing yesterday,
You will find a tomorrow.
A tomorrow promised by those gathered

Beneath This Cross.

hnc
11.5.99

Mary and Whitey lived across the street from us for thirty years. They were good neighbors and it broke my heart to hear the word cancer again. The everyday battle that is waged by a cancer victim and his or her family is amazing. The chemotherapy and radiation are only two crosses, the crosses are seeing your children's faces and watching someone you love waste away. In this household, faith was always there. It was the glue that held the tenuous house of cards from collapsing. In the months filled with doctors and what ifs, Mary's faith was stellar and still is.

I prayed even though I explained to Mary that I was not very good and maybe no one would listen. I questioned why? Whitey died while I was in Florida. I was beside myself. My responsibilities were such that I could not be there. One afternoon in the sun I wrote: **To Mary, With Love.** It was a remembrance of a friend and neighbor. I was saying good-bye.

To Mary, With Love

The quiet intelligence is gone

The unhurried smile is gone

The dropping of chin and soft chuckle, they are gone

The markings of a robust, redheaded youth are gone

The shoulders that carried the responsibility of job and family are gone

Left for us:

The love of a wonderful union

The respect of children

The beauty of grandchildren

A community's appreciation

A prosperous company

The shadow of his importance

The refrains of the laughter of friends

The memories within each heart

The fruits of his life:

Found on the plot of land, one man's life,
Coming into bloom and harvest from now unto eternity.

hnc
1.25.99

A grandson he would never meet....

I so wanted to be a friend to Robert. He missed his dear friend and wife, Patty. Flowers were her love, so I reminisced in a garden. It was difficult watching a man deal with his loss. I know that tears were shed, but not for all to see. We have only recently allowed men to cry and for it to be "all right". I know what Robert was experiencing. I asked for his friendship and was able to offer my compassion. Robert was involved in business, I envied that need to be in the office. The mind was occupied, it made the day go faster. It also made one have a focus and people to touch.

One good feature of having a friend to confide in who has lost a spouse, is the dialogue. You can talk about your mate, how you miss him or her, what you did together, the children you shared, the funny stories, and another widow or widower listens. They are not threatened by your memories. I wrote **For Robert** because I wanted him to know that others care.

For Robert......

"Patty" the voice of love spoke her name
Could a certain flower answer "yes" as memory is stirred
Could a vibrant, pungent tea rose mark the woman as she was
Never having heard her voice nor viewed her smile, I ask, maybe
The delicate sweetness of a lilac should be the choice
Better still, not one or two, but a beautiful bouquet
Each flower to be a remembrance of a special quality,
Known to only you.

Your Patty, your love, your flower garden
A garden that will understand your grief
The planting of yesterday's sharing
Allowing time to make the harvest fulfilling
This garden reaping wondrous tomorrows
This special harvest... may it yield precious peace.

A peace, I pray, to be nurtured, enjoyed and found for you and me.

....In love and understanding,

hnc
4.13.99

May Flowers   Watercolor by David Armstrong   1947-1998

Dearest David. Jim and I shared in David's life in so many ways. He and his wife, Anne, were friends of my sister and her husband. Their journey through illness and then death touched us deeply. We had been battling cancer for some time and knowing David was gone shook us to the very core, would death touch us too? I wrote a long letter to the family viewing David's wonderful accomplishment: his life.

Dave was the Dean of Students at Lafayette College in Easton, Pennsylvania. He was an accomplished businessman, an educator, an innovator in so many areas; but mostly he was a warm, loving and compassionate human being. As a tribute to the man, David A. Portlock, Lafayette College gave physical permanence to the Black Cultural Center on campus. It will forever by known as: The David A. Portlock Black Cultural Center, referred to as the BCC by all the students.

The dedication of a building in his honor at a college he loved, attended by his wife, Anne, and his children, was moving (his daughter, Laura, read his favorite poem, *If*). Jim was now gone and I had to share in the tribute, so **The House On The Corner** was my gift of understanding and pride. I attended the event and tried to lend support, but as you know, it is hard to have a heavy heart yourself and be upbeat. In this theatre it was best to say little and touch a lot.

The House On the Corner

It is just a house
Front porch, windows and shutters...
Please, open the door
No bell, no knocking...just a turn of the knob.

Take a step up...you are in BCC
The home of students who are in sync...
Students of Lafayette who care
All students of God.

The name David A. Portlock graces BCC
This home is the soul of our friend.
His legacy of fair play and deep concern
Can be felt as we stroll from room to room.

As hands are extended, eyes meet and fellowship enacted
These rooms are aglow with a certain sunset...
The sunset of days gone...days to come.
Our prayers have been answered.

David's family will always find comfort here.
Our wishes for Lafayette memories reinforced as
Warmth from smiles, answers to questions and
Brotherhood for all, can be found...

Within,

The House On the Corner

hnc
10.99

BCC Lafayette College 2001

Another death brings home the pain and suffering that we all must go through, so came the poem, **The Front Pew**. As I sat with my grief in this beautiful church, surrounded by friends and God, I looked at the empty front pew and realized that we all must occupy it one day.

Dick and Pris were very good friends. When we moved into our new town they invited us to an open house. They really had never met us, but mutual friends told them about us. What nice and thoughtful caring neighbors. Opening their home and friends to us endeared them both to us.

When I heard of another path paved with cancer, I cried. I cried not only for them and their beautiful family, but for myself and my family. I do not understand completely the emotions that death brings to the front, only that it rears its head and you must deal....so, I took to my writing and shared again thoughts and remembrances that marked my caring.

The Front Pew

It is your time.
Your hour to sit in black.
A time to feel that deep sorrow,
Looking to find a stillness,
Hoping to keep memories fresh, yet,
The finality, as you occupy that front pew.

The church silently fills.
Nods of remembrance
Embraces of friendship
Every seat marks a time
A yesterday of doing,
Still, the front pew remains empty.

Glasses perch on noses
As eyes peruse the given pamphlet.
We are here to bid a final farewell.
As time past flies through the mind's eye
Our own grief become unbearable, then,
The first pew silently becomes filled.

Music shelters those thoughts of grief,
Enabling the mind to rejoice to familiar refrains.
We stretch to see you who have loved,
We admire your courage,
We pray that being a loving family will help the pain
Of being in the front pew.

The bells ring and the vestments appear.
The book of Wisdom and the Gospel of John,
The homily of life reaching the shore.
The visualization of rhythmic waves, everyday life,
A life to celebrate, yes, the celebration of his life,
You, who are seated in the first pew.

Memories of Dick, C.D., Richard B. Thomas.
Like they happened just yesterday, always dear.
To be treasured, they were the man.
Each with their own tribute to friend and Father,
Laughter and knowing nods, directed to
His family in that front pew.

Every pew representing a time capsule.
Each friend took to remembering.
TIME, PEOPLE, MONEY memories.
Softball, basketball, golf.
Parties where stories were spun
Wagers and "I'll bet" challenges
Written on wallpaper to be recalled,
Were found in every pew, along with tears.

A voice rose and touched the soul.
A song that told of Dick's journey with Pris.
The journey of a wonderful lifetime.
The sea of contentment sailed,
The harbors of their love visited.
The solitude of a husband and wife.
To be held dear in the dark of night,
Until the light of morning arrives,

Warming you, his loved ones,
Who now occupy the front pew.

hnc
9.26.00

Chapter VI   One the Road Again, the Friendship Trail

Beginning to Share...to live again.

It was very slow in happening. I only wanted to run, to keep busy. This is very hard when you do not have a direction. Running seems to be the name of the game while experiencing that terrible feeling of grief. Time seems to be the only component that slows the pace. You will find that to be true.

All at once I realized that sharing my feelings with a friend was an easy outlet. Not long dialogues, but written words directed to them personally. I began to share what comes naturally to me, my observations. I was embarrassed that maybe my poems could not communicate and were not good. Try, try, try. I was rewarded with smiles and thank yous. See, trying harder is the answer, do not fear failure. Believe there is no room for failure between the letters:

F R I E N D.

"I love you". Spoken after so many years of marriage, not to your wife, but another, can prove to be very difficult. The anguish of being unfaithful, but the desire to live again, so **Say I Love You** was shared with the hope that light would shine upon two new friends. That wonder of dating is with us no matter what age. It is a real chore to get back into the ring and not get knocked out in the first round. If you are lucky enough to find someone who is as ethical and loving as you are, you have dodged a TKO.

Continuing the courtship will probably need the admitting that you love someone. Trying to share that feeling of love was the reason for this piece. The person experiencing grief needs to be nurtured. If saying "I love you" will help, then by all means say it. Understand that two very good friends can love.

Say I Love You

"*I Love You*".....*in so many ways three words of wonder!*
As youthful voice bespeaks, a demand for tomorrow is heard.
The middle years hear "I Love You" and you are thankful.
But, then as death silences the "I Love You" so dear.

And, you then enter the lonely time.
"I Love You" is what you want to hear again.
It will brighten the darkness......
But what demands......what promises.....what heartbreak in store.

None.......because.......
Just the words "I Love You".......
> *Should shine brilliant,*
> *Kaleidoscope a rainbow,*
> *Mark a special person........*
>> *One who cares,*
>> *One who reaches out,*
>> *One of God's children who can feel the need to love and be loved.*

No demands, no explanation, just a hand extended in loving friendship
Opening a vista of:
> *Tall mountains*
> *Gentle glens*
> *Pulsating streams*
> *Fragrant flora......and......*
> *A whispering wind on whose zephyrs can be heard the refrains of:*

"I Love You, too".

hnc
4.00

A six foot, six inch soul mate. I arrived at his door to be fed on bacon and eggs and good advice. Be myself, don't feel sorry for yourself, you were lucky to have had a love so wonderful, so, damn it, straighten up!! I said, "thank you" in the only way I could. I looked up at him and pressed **A View From Below** into his out-stretched hands.

A View From Below

He stands above the pulsating crowd
His hair of white, his athletic stride.

A caring heart beats within,
A wit, lopsided at best, shields the shadows of yesterday.

A slow pace is never noted as
Quickness of mind and body are ever present.

An unfinished word, a sentence hangs in mid air,
But a firm, loving arm reaches to enforce concern.

A new friend who is a special autumn babe
Will celebrate his birth today, a beautiful fall event.

And I will open my arms for that special hello
As I wish him all the happiness and good health he deserves.

For caring for others with calls and advice,
Perchance is called...bread upon the waters...

For his new threshold shall be filled with thankful friends
Bringing him good joy today, tomorrow and always.

And I will be forever thankful to know him
To wish him, Happy Birthday.

Fondly,

A second rate poet, a thankful friend.

hnc
9.98

We were high school buddies, I even wrote, "Remember, Helen" in his yearbook. He did, at our class reunion. Forty-five years had passed from "good-bye" to "hello, again". His natural concern for those he touches prompted him to reach out. I was wary to share my writing with one so knowledgeable, but **EHA** was received and his joy at my sharing thoughts sealed my need for this forever friend.

EHA

I watched from the foyer of the Library
The appropriate spot to see the walk, view the mannerisms.
Tall, slim with glasses perched
Briefcase tucked at an angle
Blue suit, smart tie, only fringed loafers
Questioned the full look of Mr. Chips.

So much a part of a college campus
The earned right to be there after graduation.
The importance of his mind and his always caring
Appreciated by his peers and the trustees.
The confidence of who he is and what he knows
Tells as his smile welcomes me and his hand takes mine.

He is an engineer.
The analytical answers are not far from the question
As the preciseness is not always short
And the rightness need not be argued.
Yet, never with authority that rankles
Nor uncomfort at your not understanding.

The reason....he is also a musician.
His love for and ability softens the edge.
His hands are expressive, magical fingers, soft touch.
With voice whispered in song
As music takes lead in dance
The gentleman emerges.

To watch him tackle a project
With focus and meticulous habits
It is not a wonder at success.
But what cost this success
Honestly, nothing as we can see
For this friend I find perfect.

hnc
9.99

A dear friend's Father opted to leave the hills of West Virginia and pursue a career in music. Being a coal miner would not do, but "Why?" After a deep conversation on why we take different roads and how difficult these choices are, the piece **Black Gold** found it's way into my computer. Asking questions and then finding answers, a definite road to finding relief from grief and the sadness surrounding it. After I asked, his success as a family man, a musician and a human being answered. It was his belief in his talent, in himself. You see, he did tell me.

Black Gold

Where is this place that tunnels out of sight?
How does it feel to be embraced with such blackness?
Is courage your companion? Is God your strength?
Tell me.

Does hunger motivate you?
Are responsibilities pushing you?
Does personal awareness enable you to question?
Tell me.

Can fear make the journey dangerous?
Has panic traveled with you?
Will accomplishment ease the job?
Tell me.

Do you ever see rainbows in the jet of coal?
Does the grime wash off easily?
Does your day end with a sigh?
Tell me.

Are dreams a part of your living?
Can a book cast a light?
Does love make it easier?
Tell me.

Are you happy?
Is the shoulder next to you a comfort?
What about a future?
Tell me.

Can you see daylight?
Are you able to breathe tomorrow?
Do your fingers feel today?
Tell me.

I want to know.
I want to experience through you.
I want to feel that which I have not known.
So,

Please tell me.

hnc
11.99

In the piece, **Star Gathering**, I am beginning to reach out to be a friend again to the many women in my life. It was in response to the many phone calls asking, "What can I do to help?". It was telling them that I had come far in this journey and I wanted them to know I cared about them. I was ready to join them in everyday living. Not to be so needy that I was a burden. Our friendship is again a give and take opportunity and I am able to find joy in their lives. This was a Christmas gift to those whom I hold dear.

Star Gathering

Puddled around my feet
Held tightly in my hands
Pinned loosely to my clothes
Sparkling in my hair.

They are the stars gathered today,
The memories of stars gathered yesterday,
The hope of harvesting stars tomorrow,
Gather them, let their light shine upon your dreams.

Dreams of good health
Dreams of children hugging
Dreams of caring friends
Dreams to awaken you smiling.

Hang these stars all hours of the day
Make time to gather.
Just make a wish,
Close your eyes and a star will appear.

Pluck this star from the ether.
It represents your wants, your needs.
Surround yourself with love as you
Look into the night sky.

Gather your glistening stars
Hang them proudly for all to see.
Or tuck a few for only you to know.
But, please, dear Friend, share with me,

My joy is found in the bounty of your stars.

hnc
12.22.99

That God Created A Tree is a piece that marked my seeing. Taking a class in writing was a big step in my recovery. Going out at night alone to school was a bit scary, but I did it! (You can too.) People listened to my words, commented both good and bad and I wasn't turned away. My work took on another dimension. I was able to go beyond myself and see and feel that which surrounds me. Unlike The Grey Lady that was visual, this marked my being able to dream and imagine again. When you are a dreamer as a child it never leaves you. Try dreaming and use that imagination and hang stars. On my journey I passed a tree and finally was able to hang a few stars, it felt so good.

That God Created A Tree

I stand near your kitchen window
My arms stretched to deflect the sun.
I watch as you dunk your cookies
And hear your laughter.

I listen for the bang of the door
Anticipate your arrival under my branches.
With book under arm, snack in pocket
You hide among my leaves and enjoy.

I remember the day you hung the birdhouse
The day a family of wrens arrived, and you clapped.
The squirrels you referred to as "My Neighbors".
Who constantly scampered at my feet.

I felt your tears as you cuddled in my branches
And nursed your bruised knees.
The sharing of secrets with that special friend
And the giggles that were muffled.

I have enjoyed winter
Watching snowmen march in the yard.
The feel of Spring rains enchanting
As you "oh and ah" the arrival of daffodils.
My importance reaches its peak in summer
As my shade guards you as you play house.

I will always wear the brilliance of Autumn
Remember you snuggling, safe from frost
Your blonde curls tucked into your baseball cap,
Now falling to your shoulders as you run to maturity.

Please come home soon
I will await your return, as do your loved ones.
And I am forever grateful to have shared and watched
But also grateful,

That God created a tree.

hnc
10.31.99

Spring Passage Oil by David Armstrong 1947-

To Give, March Winds and **A Smile** were written to be in newsletters sent from Hill House, a warm and caring home for elderly citizens. I was asked to be on the board with the sole purpose of editing the writing for their newsletter. I was starting to give and contribute again. After making a promise to help others and maybe find my own value again, these pieces are very important. Contributing to a good cause in my own words, you can feel the gaining of confidence and the lessening of grief. By doing I was being healed.

To Give

It started with a penny
Dreaming of candy
Yet disappearing into a small cloth bag for the poor.

The nickels, dimes and quarters
Saved for a day at the fair
But jingling into a can marked "War Effort".

Dollars stuffed in a mayo jar
Earmarked for that special something
Finding its way into college coffers.

"The Fund" established by
Young adults planning
Was divided as community needs arise.

Finally "The Fund" grew
And the family voted
Upon the charity of its choice.

A legacy......yes....
As family shared and cared
The joy of giving taught to another generation.

hnc
9.14.99

March Winds

They come without warning.
A whistle marks their arrival.
Your window rattles and
The trees are blown, no leaves to take.
Your hat is held tightly, that could go.
The March winds are upon us.

Gone are the February snows.
The ice has melted and run away.
Temperatures fell, as did spirits.
No walk today, dear feet.
Dark clouds visited our House on the Hill.
How fast they now travel, March winds are here.

Button up, errands to run.
Swirls of leaves, eddies of current
Announce the presence of March.
A crocus breaks through the soil.
It cries for the garden to awaken
It feels the March wind beckon a bloom.

Spring is in the air.
Just maybe in your hope.
The thought of basking in the sun.
Sweater, for sure, why not?
Joyful memories of Springs afar.
Brought to this House on the Hill.

So, come March Winds.
Join us for lunch.
Partake in dinner.
Enjoy our creative prowess.
Laugh and share our laughter.
For Spring will arrive soon,

On the gusts of the Winds of March!

hnc
2.22.00

A Smile

It starts at the corner of the mouth
It grows bigger and larger every second
It bypasses the nose, causing a few twitches
Arrives at the eyes with gusto!

Soft folds surround the eyes
Expressing their delight.
A twinkle of green, blue, gray or brown
Shoots from the iris, saying hello.

Not a word is spoken.
Just a face filled with friendship.
Reaching across the span
To touch, quietly touch you.

A gift, a special something.
To know that you are seen.
To feel a caring for you alone
And then it begins,

At the corners of your mouth
Reaching your eyes.
Responding to the gesture
You return this greeting,

With a smile of your own.

hnc
8.13.00

Chapter VII   A Memorable Venue

Sports are my love. I have always thought that the ability to participate and do well in athletics was a special talent. I was reminded of my joy in seeing young people perform during this special football season. I was beginning to enjoy again, even though I do still miss Jim during events that were meaningful to us. So after a very impressive awarding of my husband's scholarship at the annual football banquet, I sent **A Special Season** as a thank you to the coaches and parents who were responsible for the evening. That night and its activities made me feel a part of the world again. This football program is special because of our family's involvement. Being able to participate was a way of continuing to touch my husband's love of football. The lesson here is that even though your loved one is gone, you still share his interests and therefore feel his presence.

A Special Season

State Champs
State Champions
The 1999 Team
The young men of Autumn.

With names like Henry, Plagianakos, Taylor, Aksoz,
Finn, Cuartas, Sternbergh, Timchak, Wellington,
Bordeaux, Grosz, May, Imbrogno, Sullivan and Bastis
Young men of America.

Coach's mentoring
Discussions on and off the field
Bruises, pain, rote and camaraderie
Strengthen a team of young men.

Hopes and fears
Wishes and dreams
Reality and fantasy
Each to his own as they take the field, these young men.

The anxiety of doing battle evident.
Rhythmic scuffling of cleated feet.
Last minute checks as to equipment and attitude.
Then, between the goal posts these young men jog.

Each week has a special personality.
Each opposing team its own character
Each play to be executed as practiced
Young men and coaches striving for the win.

What worked?
What were our strengths?
Next week's opponents Achilles' heel?
Sorting every man's proven team contribution for a chance at the
States.

Success can be felt
The playing field to test your talent
A prayer to gain confidence
Young men embrace as they play their last game together.

Four quarters, flags, formations, fumbles, forward passes,
Half time, the band, the cheerleaders, the fans,
The score board records
A game well played, these State Champs!

A season of Saturdays completed,
Filmed with the purpose of preserving
The roar of the crowd, the thrill of the game
To savor the yesterdays of some talented young men of Greenwich.

They have journeyed to this table
From every corner of this town.
They wear the mantles of family tradition and values
But, they dress alike, these men with different numbers.

Now only wonderful memories of a season ended.
Gathered with family and friends
A night of awards and thank you's
As young men gather to be honored.

Trophies still have meaning
Certificates will be mounted
Nicknames never to be forgotten
Scholarships, records, accomplishments of Cardinals.

Coaches giving personal insights
Mothers shedding tears and Fathers aglow with pride.
The brotherhood of football in its finest hour
Etching memories never to be forgotten, young men.

The family of football and home entwined
The touching with arms and speech
The reason for a season, not the score,
To make ready for tomorrow, these young men of today.

hnc
12.11.99

Chapter VIII   A Rest Stop

At this point in time I saw the sunshine, and maybe a rainbow or two. While listening to a sermon on who is responsible for the keeping of a promise, these words spun out and at this point my promise was to try harder to get well. I had started to question those around me and my own commitment to others. Everything was timely. So came, **Listen, A Promise** and the heartfelt desire to be whole again.

Listen, A Promise

From the podium
A promise of freedom.
From the altar
A promise of faithfulness.
From a handshake
A promise of honesty.
From the heart
A promise of love.

So easily spoken,
So easy to implement,
So easy to chart,
So easy to evaluate,
So easy to offer,
So easy to hear,
So easy to use,
So easy to gain access.

Your promise has gained entry.
To a political position
To a marriage
To a business deal
To a friendship
To a group
To a feeling of contentment,
You are there on a promise.

Then, it becomes more than euphoria,
It takes on responsibility.
It becomes a task at times.
It may reap not one new harvest.
It darkens your doorway.
It causes you to fall out of formation.
It deals you hardship.
It causes you pain.

This, this wonderful, hopeful promise.
Why? You ask.
Why? You wonder.
Why? You lament.
Why? You curse.
Why? You cry!
Why me?
Because you made that promise.

Make the promise,
In the company of others
Into your pillow
To the stars
To your loved ones
To your contemporaries
To your God
To your reflection.

Who must hear?
Who will remember?
Who will hold you to this promise?
Who will profit from it?
Who will be made happier because of it?
Whose life will be fuller?
What smile will be brighter?
Will your promise make a difference?

Yes, maybe briefly to those you touch,
Forever for you, the road you travel is yours,
Traveled, fueled by your voiced promise,
For you to execute
For you to understand
For you to jump the hurdles to deliver
For you to carry to completion
Yours alone on its journey.

A true promise is spoken silently
Even though others hear it.
It is spoken because you believe
Believe you can make a difference.
So believing, you must now try
Try to see this promise evolve
See this promise become reality
A reality only you have promised.

Easier to close your eyes and deny.
Easier to let go.
Easier to walk away.
Easier to blame others.
Easier to fall into despair.
Easier to not remember.
Easier to forget.
Easiest, never to promise.

No, promises are easy.
Integrity is hard.
Promises make for laughter
Fulfilling them gives joy.
Grandstanding feeds egos
Quiet satisfaction banquets the heart.
Deathside promises are forever
Not two, just one who will always remember.

Softly make that important promise.
Tenderly utter the words of promise.
Look into the eyes of that special someone.
Understand the impact of your action,
The responsibility of your words
The essence of a promise.
For you are now bound,
Bound to that promise.

For only you need heed, for reality promises:
Your heart is the one to break
Your soul will be the one to deal
Your smile may disappear
Your step may falter
Your speech becomes stilted
Your promise is spoken
And your destiny is in your words.

hnc
2.21.00

Chapter IX   Memory Lane

Then death again appeared on my doorstep. My Mother died the day after Christmas, 1999. Her death stunned me. I now saw my Father as I had been just such a short time ago. I held his hand and cried. This wonderful woman who loved me so, gone? Yes, just when I thought I could stand alone, I was brought to my knees again. So I poured my heart out in her **Eulogy**, to be shared with those who loved her. My writing was a source of consolation.

My Father and I went to Florida in early January, Mother was not with us on the trip, but as we entered the gate I knew she would always be with me. **A Gardenia** tells the story.

Two days later my dear Father was rushed to the hospital. My world stopped. I anguished over our plight. My son showed his love by flying down immediately and my family sent messages from afar. **His Hands**, a piece about my Father, was born of despair and hope. At this time I wrote as a postscript: This morning my Mother is gone and my Father lays critically ill and my heartbreaks. Do you sometimes wonder at the possibility of a broken heart?

My Mother 1935

Eulogy

She was a small blonde babe
Her foot held delicately during a family portrait due to a sore toe.
Around her the family posed
Small elegant emigrants, faces of angels
Sternness by need, blue eyes, well-waxed mustache,
Fair of skin, religiously focused, bi-lingual
A family soon to be parted.

Her mother's death on Christmas Eve
The scattering of siblings into the arms of Mother Church
Three daughters, five sons and a husband burdened
With a promise to educate, the only way to survive, education.
A husband's promise kept, graduations.
Family held in her heart, this daughter touched them always,
This beautiful woman fearlessly traveling a new road.

The love, the passion and an elopement were to mold the next 65 years.
Her determination, his work ethic.
Her need for family, his need for her.
His common sense, her dreams.
The meeting of every day head-on as times dictated.
Not always together, but never, no never really apart.
The birth of two daughters, a family complete.

Her books, her friends, her politics, her far flung siblings,
Her Helen Marie, His Virginia...Butch.
But, all four formed a union never to be questioned.
Love was the mainstay, education the answer, an open mind of a liberated woman.
Her tools forged by the Sisters of Mercy, her application unique, her own.
And he always by her side to provide.
Love served at every meal, not always words, just love.

Home, it was not true that you can never return home,
For we were always welcome, our visits anticipated,
The blue Christmas tree, to remind us of the Virgin Mary
The prayers before a meal, to the clink of settling forks,
The presents of rosary beads, statues, strains of hymns from music boxes,
Pictures of children, grandchildren, great grandchildren,
Positioned next to our "Polish" Pope, Saints to keep them safe and medals from youth.

She never questioned her faith, her church was her friend.
It proved to be her sustenance, her family her raison d'etre.
But, the union of marriage was her chalice.
From this goblet ran the very essence of her daily life.
Happiness surrounded the aroma of cooking, His.
Accomplishment in the clicking of needles, Hers.
They marked the years as time seemed to know no end.

Nell, then Mom, then Nanny, then Nanny Napoli.
She was known to answer to every one.
Her grandchildren received letters with enclosed stamps,
Packages of bologna and cheese were shared in dorm rooms.
Acey Nellie made you laugh at the pinochle table.
Cartwheels accented the picnics of their youth.
Stories, this day, shared.

Her grandchildren could always find a listening ear.
But, beware if you were to open the refrigerator too often.
Generous as college tuitions were needed,
But, you must always save for a rainy day.
Quietly waiting in these last years for help
Never having to wait long, for he was there.
A silhouette of two people, as they walked down the lane.

A darkened silhouette of aging parents holding each other
Lightening as great grandparents tend their flock.
Opaque with love for the grandchildren
Clear in their devotion to their daughters
Dazzling with their love and respect for sons-in-law.
Translucent as young parents
Brilliant as young lovers.

A silhouette to remind us that life begins again.
Her life is here before you.
Her life is within us all.

We love you.

hnc
12.28.99

A Gardenia

It bloomed anticipating our arrival
Our arrival from the frosty North
A time of sadness and good-byes
Four dozen gardenias above her casket
Their aroma never to be forgotten
Remembered as we entered the courtyard.

Twelve years entering this courtyard, this month
Yet, never a bloom, always after our leave.
My Mother's favorite flower, every holiday upon her bosom.
Planted in the courtyard, planning a bloom for her arrival
Just wanting to show my love
Wanting to show my sameness in my love of gardenias.

Never to walk with me into this home
Never to accept the florist box
Never to touch me again, no sign of love
Yet, one single gardenia, a fragrant greeting
And she stood beside me as I walked
Took my hand as I plucked one single bloom.

Tears watered its whiteness
Hopefully to bloom forever by my bedside
Its fragrance to rock me to sleep
Memories to permeate my dreams
Questions swirl as I ask how and why now
Blooming for the first time, never for her to see.

It has been four days since our arrival
My Father is ill, his grief so sad.
The bloom is yellowing in its cradle
Pollinating the air as I enter and leave
A reminder of her presence
A tribute to her love.

A new bloom has appeared on the bush.
I feel it represents tomorrow
A tomorrow without her kisses and hugs.
This bloom will also die by my bedside
Another to take its place until the season ends.
Until my season ends.

hnc
1.9.00

His Hands

I was aware of his hands
The respirator hissed
The nurse quietly worked
The hospital surrounding us
A son to comfort me, yet
All I can envision are his hands.

These hands try to shake the bonds.
These hands clench and unclench.
The eyes are not aware of me.
His hands are my only link.
The square cut nails, forever spotless,
The strength so evident in their shape.

I remember these hands bathing me
Remember these hands on my forehead,
"No fever, Nell, she is getting well."
These hands buckling my first skates
Attending to my hands on the bat,
Throwing the ball, cradling my doll.

Expressive in speech
Competent in affection
Experienced in culinary arts
Knowingly tender with my babies
Herculean in strength
Authoritative to his family.

They were up to every task.
A wonder as he combed his beautiful hair, often.
A tool as hard work demanded ungodly tasks.
A bond when extended to others.
A refuge for emotion.
An outlet for anger.

My fear of never holding these hands
A fear of losing their touch
Personal fear of mortality.
Afraid to let go of yesterday.
Can I stand the pain of goodbye?
So, I hold his hand and pray.

The respirator is silenced.
The hands are unbound.
The eyes reach out to me.
But it is the hand, that I take
The hand that comforts me.
Those hands so dearly loved,

Thank God there will be tomorrow.

hnc
1.29.00

My Father's hands.....May 200(

Chapter X   *Down the Mountain, Into a Valley*

The Merry-Go-Round marked a real turning point in my grief process. I was shocked by the news that someone I had loved had announced his engagement. I felt so rejected. Knowing that you are now reaching out to others and are not so alone helped a tad. But when you are hurt because of an incident that was not foreseen, it is fine to be upset. What is not fine is when it knocks you off your track to becoming whole again! I felt so unnerved and then I realized that this was a step I could take to understand that not everything will be as you want it. Get on the merry-go-round and experience life again, not wait for life to take care of me......the world is yours, go for it!

Photo taken by Kelly Smith

The Merry-Go-Round

I can hear the calliope, feel
The excitement of the minute
The apprehension of the ride
The total enjoyment of experiencing.

With no one at my side, I approach,
Is it slowing just for me?
I look to the attendant for direction,
Am rewarded with only the double clang.

The ride is to begin.
I take that first step, measured with the movement,
Aboard, I try to get my bearings.
Where to turn, where to light?

With anxiety I reach out to the animals.
They are silent, their eyes just stare at me.
I become frightened, and bolt to a bench
Where I sit and view my surroundings.

The world around me is filled with wonder
The world outside is a blur.
The music begins, the motor hums
And I am on my maiden voyage.

It was safer to sit alone, hands in lap
As the speed increased
As the music becomes faster
As the atmosphere becomes a retreat.

Then the knowing of what was aboard.
I have been here before.
A time remembered
A time cherished.

But not on this bench.
Perhaps on the beautiful swan.
Take yourself in hand
Perch on its back and ride.

But then what about that stallion?
The fierceness in his eyes attract.
Can I climb upon his back?
Can I hang on as he runs and rears to the music?

It is a joyous ride.
A ride with concern
A ride that exhilarates
But is it what you remembered?

Then you see it, the ring.
You cannot reach it from the Stallion
You cannot reach it from the Swan
You cannot reach it from the bench

You must stand on your own feet,
Hold onto the Merry-Go-Round post,
Listen to the song of the calliope
And use your judgment, go to the edge!

When do I lean?
How far out do I dare reach?
Must I know the speed at which I travel?
Judgment supreme, can I do this?

"Try," yells the watchful elephant.
"Careful," warns the soulful donkey.
"Good luck," smiles the beautiful gelding.
"Yes," I reply as I ready myself.

The first step, taken.
The position, my own.
The need, a reality
The ring approaches...

I grab, and I miss.
Will there be another chance?
Yes, around I go
I grab, success, a ring!

My elation is short lived.
The ring is brass.
I instinctively know it is not right.
But, why, have I been here before?

I know. It must be gold.
There is a gold ring among the brass.
Try again.
Another brass catch.
Try again.
The music hesitates
The motor beats through your souls
The animals hold their breaths.

Gold? No, another brass ring.
Will experience be the key?
How many more tries?
How many more brass rings?

The tears of frustration and hurt clear my vision.
I see the joy of reaching
I see the joy of being
I feel the joy of revolving with the merry-go-round.

You are fortunate to be within the sound of calliope
You should be grateful for your reach
Grateful for the coin to purchase this ride
Grateful for you, for your ability to stand, to hold on.

So sings the music.

Reach for the ring,
Brass or gold, it is now.
Someday you may again find a gold ring,
A gold ring that you may keep, that may be yours.

Until, then, enjoy.
Listen to the music
Touch the animals with love.
Rejoice, this is your time.

So sing the lyrics of within.

Soon, the calliope will run down
The world outside will be visible
The arm holding the rings will retract
But before that double clang:

Be thankful for this chance at the golden ring,
Be thankful for the friends touched on your journey to the edge,
Be thankful you reached for the ring, either brass or gold,
Be thankful of the time and love needed to build and share this wonder,

Your Merry-Go-Round!

So sings reality.

hnc
2.10.00

I Arrived On Wounded Wings was the phoenix arising from the ashes. I felt so enlightened with my writing, I wonder if that is healthy. I thought, "this is good", I felt as though I had turned a corner, I was on the street where I have always lived....the place where I could be my own best friend, and love being just me. I now know I can fly again.

I Arrived on Wounded Wings

Hold out your hands
I must retreat into their comfort.
My wounds are many.
Though your eyes may not see
I know your heart feels.
I must rest.

The journey of these past three years,
They have caused fatigue and uncertainty.
My defenses are down
My vulnerability evident.
My head is lowered
My future only a guess.

Please, I beg, be my friend.
My song is gone,
Listen to my eyes.
The shine of my wings
Now a dull luster.
My being is in distress.

Then a touch filled with concern,
A voice of tenderness,
Smiles of encouragement,
Words of wisdom,
Genuine caring,
A rainbow reflected on thunderclouds.

A cozy nest in which to heal,
It's name, friendship.
An ear to listen,
In the name of friendship.
Tears spilled, understanding
The need for friendship.

Seconds, minutes, hours of questioning.
Weeks, months, years of pain.
Time will heal says the world.
Please make it soon says I.
To sleep the time away
To heal in the ether of dreams,

Not alone, in the hands of a friend.,
In the bosom of caring.
On the waves of voice,.
By the written word.
A beribboned gift, so special,
Because someone cared.

Sun, moon, stars,
I can see again.
The darkness is not so frightening.
Hands, arms, warm faces,
I can feel again.
Awareness of a forever friend.

I begin to emerge.
My feathers glow from care.
My wings mended with love.
My eyes glisten with happiness.
My body responds with joy.
Can I fly again? I ask.

Try, try those wings.
Look at the horizon.
Find the sun.
Soar to new heights.
View new venues.
For you are well.

I know with all my soul
That the pain is still there.
That the memories will sooth
That what was, still is.
That I have so much,
At times almost too much.

I must fly.
I must soar solo.
My feathers preened
My mind clear and loving
My hands held in prayer
Thanking you, dear friend.

Never be far from me.
Always reach out to me.
Understand my flight.
Do not worry of my plight.
Listen for my song,
It is sung for your ears alone.

Its lyrics praise your goodness,
Thank you, Friend.

hnc
3.26.00

Chapter XI   Enjoying the Fall Leaves

Laughter and a slap to the thigh and not to the head!

I really find these three pieces hilarious. I laughed so hard after I had written them. To laugh again is such a good place to stop, so enjoy and, please, know that you can laugh again......know that I am here to talk to, just read what I have written......it was meant to be shared, it was written so you could relate, so that you know you are not alone.

He Did It!! was the first of my pieces that made me laugh. I almost could feel the tension leave my fingers as I typed what had transpired. What had happened is a dear friend shaved off his beard of twenty-five years. It tickled my funny bone to hear him tell me what he had done over the phone. His voice and maybe his Doubting Thomas attitude prompted a response. It is good to laugh, it is good to share laughter, and it is good to hear yourself laugh. Try it, you WILL like it, you have earned it!

He did it!!

Can you believe he did it?
Can you believe he did it?
No, but he did it.
He really did it!

I wonder if any hesitation was evident.
Did the eyes in the mirror register remorse?
Did the hand shake a wee bit?
Did resolve make it steady as one goes?

The first step taken, a gasp heard.
The second phase underway, a slight smile.
A final swipe and mission completed.
He did it!

The weapon lays forgotten.
The reflection undaunted.
The hand moves to feel.
The fingers are rewarded.

He did it!
I missed being there.
I missed the unveiling.
I missed twenty-five years of coverage. I feel regret
That I was not there
I want to touch.
I want to see what he did.

But, he did it!
Then he called and said, "guess what",
"I did it."
Then he laughed.........

His laughter shared the deed.
His wonder made me warm all over.
His need to feel younger amazed me.
His coldness made me want to administer.

But, he did it!
He did it and he was glad.
He did it and he was happy.
He did it and he sounded young.

Thank you taking me with you.

hnc
12.26.99

Forgetting an appointment at any point in your life is embarrassing, but when you are in need of another invitation it can be fatal! I found I had encountered a definite senior moment. Having completely forgotten a dinner invitation I pondered how to set it right. Again, turning to my writing and having confidence in my ability to communicate, **I'm Late, I'm Late** even told of the menu for the evening. Being late isn't so bad, that's if you don't make it a habit. Starting your journey a little late is better than not starting at all. Please begin.

I'm Late, I'm Late

For a very important date,
No time to say "hello", "good-bye",
I'm late, I'm late.
I'm in a boeuf bourguignon stew.

The time is past for small repast
The soup cups filled to brim.
The tabled chair is void of guest
Where, oh where can she be?

With her mind gone silent
And her focus not keen
She has wandered from here to there.
Oh where, oh where can she be?

Hostess gracious, host with a song,
They await this tardy lass.
Invited folk are engaged in chatter
The lass engaged not at all.

Then lightning strikes, a call is made
The contact made at last.
Amazement, regret, total embarrassment
No time to primp, just hurry, hurry.

Quietly approach the guests amassed,
A hug, a shrug, a sheepish grin
Two friends with hospitality grand,
Bring on the food, the entertainment!

The evening is a gourmet's treat.
The sounds of night accent speech.
Finding like friends, know them well.
A wonder, remembering places visited.

Time to go, fully sated.
Embarrassment passed into ether.
Warmth and friendship abound.
No longer late, For This Very Important Date.

Thank you.

hnc
4.13.00

You will find that during your journey that maybe you will gain or lose weight, hair, or maybe brain cells. Whatever you lose, please view it with humor. You cannot change that which has occurred during this journey, but you can sure as hell laugh about it. This piece was a product of a weight gain and not being in control of my eating. I held that grapefruit and smiled. Walked to the computer and wrote, in script, **Ode To A Grapefruit**. I belly laughed with a friend and knew the last line to be all right!!!!

Ode to a Grapefruit

As I press the knife into the orb
As I watch the juice run from the puncture
As I smell the pungent odor
Why, am I reminded of wisdom and virtue?

Can this yellow fellow from a tree
Immortalize such a basic function
That of understanding wisdom at its purest
Being able to turn wisdom into virtue?

At the crossroad of today
When Oreo cookies call from depths well known
Can the wisdom of right turn into virtue of good
Or will the Oreos win and so exit virtue?

The wisdom is so obvious
Calories produce fat.........
Grapefruit can become virtuous
Imagine a virtuous citrus!

Did the fruit fall not far from the tree?
Did the wisdom of procreation mark its entry?
Or did it fall unheard and unheralded
To virtuously be held by myself this sunny day?

How can one small fruit represent:
The principal of wisdom and virtue?
Easy, in order to find the virtue
You must first obtain and respect wisdom.

So, exit the Oreos and the hiding fudge.
The cogent wisdom gathered
Virtue is at hand............

Cut the fucking grapefruit!!!!!

hnc
3.27.00

Chapter XII   A New Journey Begins

These following two pieces, **September 30, 2000,** and
At The Crossroad are very important for you to
study. I say so many introspective observations
about how I feel now and how I hope to deal with the
future. It is a vision of health and happiness resting
against the trama of grief. Your importance to your-
self and those around you must be felt, reach out.

September 30, 2000

It has been three years since my husband, Jim, died. As I walked this a.m. my thoughts were of him and our life together. I asked myself, "What after three years of grieving and trying to find a life alone, was our marriage and friendship all about?"

I want to say it was loving, which is true, but when I am asked to define "love" I am at a loss for words. Three years ago it would have been easy. Words like touching, caring, worrying, helping, sharing, being together would rush from my lips. Realizing, as I read those words, they are all in the here and now, Jim is not. So, my love has to change, it does not have to go away, just change. So I now must focus on what is left of that love, what special aspect of my life with Jim will carry with me as I go forward.

Memories of good times seem to surface. I will cherish these. In the poem, "A Rose" I mention the flowers of our union, our grandchildren, loving them is important. My respect and love of my children is still paramount. I step back and wonder about the other emotions that have sprung from my marriage. Importance leaps at me!

I was important to Jim. His respect of my opinions and thoughts was paramount in our relationship. He sometimes would call my projects, follies, but always with encouragement and pride, when they worked!! It was fun, it was wonderful, it was true to life....for it was not perfect. Bottom line, that word important.

I am alone now, alone with family and friends. Where has my importance gone? It has not. As I walked today, this third anniversary, I felt the need to reflect. I found I was reflecting differently, I was looking backward and ahead at the same time. I am important, not only to my family and friends, but a realization that I am important to myself.

"How?" I ask. I have an importance in the guise of a need to be productive. To be giving and caring to not only myself, but to those I come in contact with everyday. Never in a negative manner, that deletes your importance (there are words for these intentions), but to have a positive impact on this world. It dawned on me that I feel I have something to offer, myself and my abilities. At 60 plus I am still able to contribute, that makes me important to myself.

I am thankful for a thought process that enables me to see myself as important. I am thankful for the time in history when a woman is viewed as an asset for her mind and ability to organize. I am thankful that my world was filled with love. I am thankful that I can continue to love, to love with the understanding of what went before and to love with the belief that I am still important, important to me.

October 1, 2000............a new journey begins.

hnc

At The Crossroad

My journey is far from over. I have mountains and valleys to find and enjoy. I know that at times I will not have a vehicle on which to travel. The wheels will come off and I will need to ask for help in reattaching them. Being lost can happen, and then directions must be sought. All this can happen if you believe. You ask, "How can I believe again?" The answer is, "Please believe, just try, you can do it!"

I know how hard the journey will be for you, walked in shoes worn through the "soul" and untied most of the time. Not easy, but you are worth every step of healing necessary to end the painful part of your journey.

Take that first step. Take it with your own creativity, with your own speed. This is your life. You have not died. You must live on as a tribute to the life that has ended, that life that was so much you. Find peace and happiness, you deserve to live again in a place that is sunny and filled with love.

Now take my hands. Give them permission to hug you. Always remember I have been there, and I have survived.

hnc
5.25.00